Does it attract?

All about magnetic materials

Jenny Vaughan
Experiments by Meredith Blakeney

FRANKLIN WATTS
LONDON·SYDNEY

First published in 2009
by Franklin Watts

Copyright © Franklin Watts 2009

Franklin Watts
338 Euston Road
London NW1 3BH

Franklin Watts Australia
Level 17/207 Kent Street
Sydney, NSW 2000

Series editor: Sarah Peutrill
Art director: Jonathan Hair
Design: Elaine Wilkinson
Photographs: Paul Bricknell (unless otherwise credited)

Picture credits: Getty images: 17. istock photos: 9b (Jeffrey Smith), 27t (Thomas Hottner). Shutterstock: 5t (Morgan Lane Photography), 8tr (Elena Talberg), 8bl (Tomasz Trojanowski), 9tl (J Kitan), 9tr (Polina Lobanova), 14 (Awe Inspiring Images), 16br (payee), 24bl (Natalia Bratslavlev), 24tr (Switch), 25t (Stefan Ataman), 28 (Peter Elvidge), 29b (Alexandru), 29t (Yegar Korzh). SPL: 15t (Pascal Goetgheluck), 20 (Science Source), 21b (Pasieka), 21t (Cordelia Molloy), 25b (Mehan Kulyk), 26 (Andy Crump). Wishlist images: 6, 7
Cover images: Shutterstock: tl (Polina Lobanova), tr (Joanne Harris and Daniel Bubnich), r (Michelle D. Milliman), b (Ingvar Tjostheim). Every attempt has been made to clear copyright. Should there be any inadvertent omission please apply to the publisher for rectification.

With thanks to our models: Megan Collier, Lily Cornelius, Jody Humphries, Connor Rose

Dewey number: 538

ISBN: 978 0 7496 8722 9

Printed in China

Franklin Watts is a division of Hachette Children's Books, an Hachette UK company.

www.hachette.co.uk

Contents

The topics highlighted above are investigations you can try.

Words in bold are in the glossary on page 30.

What are magnetic materials?

We say materials are magnetic if they can be made into magnets, or if they are attracted to magnets.

What is a magnet?

A magnet is made of metal, or a material containing metal. Magnets can attract some other metal objects. This means they draw the objects towards themselves. Magnets can be in many shapes. Most are short bar magnets or 'U'-shaped horseshoe magnets.

Magnets come in many shapes and sizes.

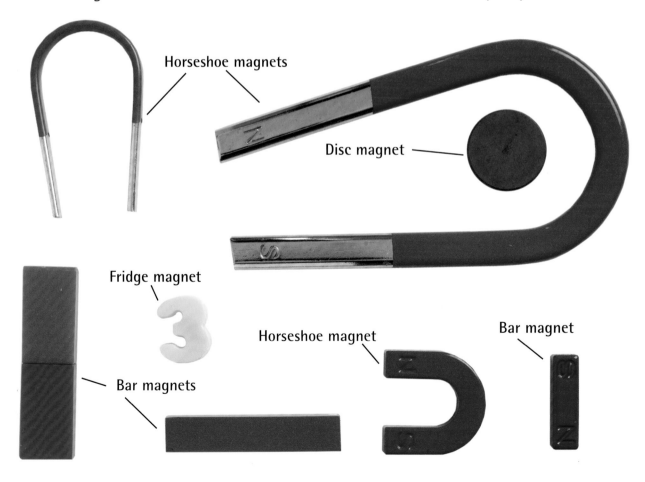

Horseshoe magnets

Disc magnet

Fridge magnet

Bar magnets

Horseshoe magnet

Bar magnet

Magnetic metals

When a material acts as a magnet, we say it has been 'magnetised'. The magnets used in the experiments in this book are all made from iron or steel. (Steel is mainly made of iron.) A few other metals can also be magnetised.

Magnetism

We can use magnets to pick up small pieces of iron, steel, nickel or cobalt. These are all magnetic materials. Magnets will stick to surfaces made from these. A magnet's power is called 'magnetism'. Magnetism is a force – something that has the power to push or pull.

Magnets can attract objects made of iron or steel, such as pins, as well as nickel and cobalt – but few other materials.

See which surfaces you can get a fridge magnet to stick to. If it sticks to a surface, you will know that the surface contains iron, steel or another magnetic material.

Note: take care not to stick a magnet to anything electronic, such as a computer, as this can damage it.

Is it magnetic?

You will need:

A magnet, some small metal objects, such as paperclips, metal teaspoons and small coins; other objects that are not made of metal, such as a plastic pen, a pencil; a sheet of paper, a thin sheet of card, a yoghurt pot of water.

To find which materials are magnetic, and which are not try this easy test.

Make a collection of small materials you plan to test. Place them on a sheet of paper.

Try picking up the objects with a magnet. Which will it pick up? Which will it not pick up? How many metal objects can your magnet hold all at once?

You will find out that the magnet attracts some materials, and not others. It will not attract anything that has no metal in it. You will also find there are many metal objects it will not pick up. The magnet may pick up some coins, but not others, because not all coins contain magnetic materials.

Choose a magnetic object and see if the magnet works through paper, and then the card. Try it with the other magnetic objects.

Put some small magnetic objects, such as paperclips, in a yoghurt pot with water in it. Lower a magnet over the objects, without touching them. Will the magnet work through water, and make the objects leap up towards it?

What happens?

Try the same experiment with magnets of different shapes and sizes. Which magnet picks the most things up? That one is the strongest.

Magnets in our everyday lives

There are magnets and magnetic materials all around us in our homes and in places where people work. They are used in many different ways.

Holding things together

Magnets are useful in fridges and freezers. There is magnetic material inside the seal around the doors. Magnetism holds the doors tightly closed. Magnets can hold handbags and briefcases closed, or knives safely to a wall.

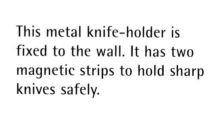

This metal knife-holder is fixed to the wall. It has two magnetic strips to hold sharp knives safely.

The magnetic strip around a fridge door is attracted to another strip around the door opening. Together, they hold the door tightly shut, but not so tightly that the door cannot be opened.

Many handbags and briefcases have magnets in their fasteners, to keep them closed.

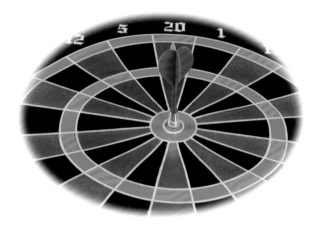

Magnets and machines

Credit and debit cards and other cards have plastic strips that contain a pattern of tiny magnets. These are set out as a code that the card reader can read. There are also magnets in the hard disks in computers, and in other kinds of **electronic equipment**.

This darts game uses magnets. The dart board is made of magnetic material. Darts made with magnets stick to it.

IMPORTANT NOTICE: Keep magnets away from credit cards. They can damage them so that they stop working.

The magnetic strip is along the underside of a credit card.

How magnets work

The two ends of a magnet are called its **poles**. A magnet has a north pole and a south pole. The magnetism is strongest at the poles. Bar magnets often have the poles marked with different colours.

These metal objects are attracted to the ends of the magnet.

Attraction and repelling

Both poles of a magnet will attract objects made from magnetic materials. When you put two magnets together, the north and south poles attract each other strongly. However, two north poles, or two south poles, will not be attracted at all. Instead, they **repel** (drive away) each other.

North and south poles attract each other – but two north poles or two south poles will repel each other.

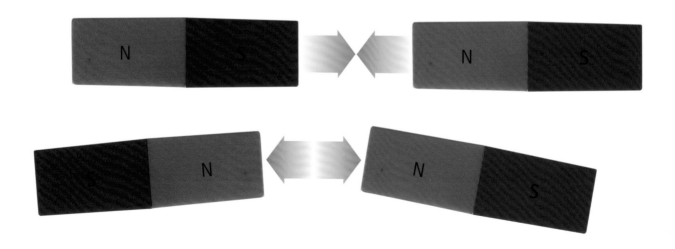

How it works

Inside a piece of magnetic material there are millions of areas of magnetism, called **domains**. They are like tiny magnets. Normally, they all point in different directions, and do not have enough strength to attract or repel anything. In a magnet, they are all lined up and pull together. They exert a strong magnetic force. If you heat a magnet, or drop it, or hit it, the domains get mixed up. The magnetic force is lost.

Push two north poles of two bar magnets together. Can you feel them repelling each other? Turn them around. What happens? Try pushing two horseshoe magnets together. Turn one of these around. What happens?

Magic paperclip

See how a magnet can make a paperclip stand up on a piece of string. It can do this if the paperclip is made of magnetic material, such as steel.

You will need:

Cotton thread; a strong, small bar magnet; a steel paperclip; a jar with a plastic lid or big see-through yoghurt pot (500 ml – big enough to get your hand inside), with its lid; sticky tape.

Cut the thread a little longer than the jar measures top to bottom. Tie the paperclip to one end of the thread. Tape the other end to the bottom of the jar (inside). The string and the paperclip together should be a tiny bit shorter than the length of the jar.

Turn the jar upside down. The paperclip hangs downwards. This is because a force the Earth exerts, called gravity, is pulling it.

Tape the magnet inside the lid of the jar.

Place the lid on the jar and, once again, turn it upside down so that the paperclip hangs from the string. It must be very nearly touching the magnet.

Carefully turn the jar right side up. Normally, the paperclip falls to the bottom of the jar. But if the clip is close to the magnet, the magnet's force will pull it upwards. It is stronger than the force of gravity.

Undo the lid. How far away from the paperclip can you move the magnet before the paperclip falls away?

Now try this

Tie a thread to a paperclip. Tape the other end of the thread to a table. Use a magnet to see if you can hold the paperclip in the air without touching it.

Magnetic field

The area around a magnet where it exerts its force is called its **magnetic field**. The magnet attracts any magnetic materials inside the field.

Iron filings

Tiny pieces of iron called **iron filings** can show how a magnetic field works. In the picture, there is a magnet on a piece of paper. Iron filings have been sprinkled around it. If the paper is gently shaken, the filings move in the magnetic field. They form a pattern of lines in the field. Scientists call these 'lines of force'.

Iron filings can be used to show the lines of force around a magnet.

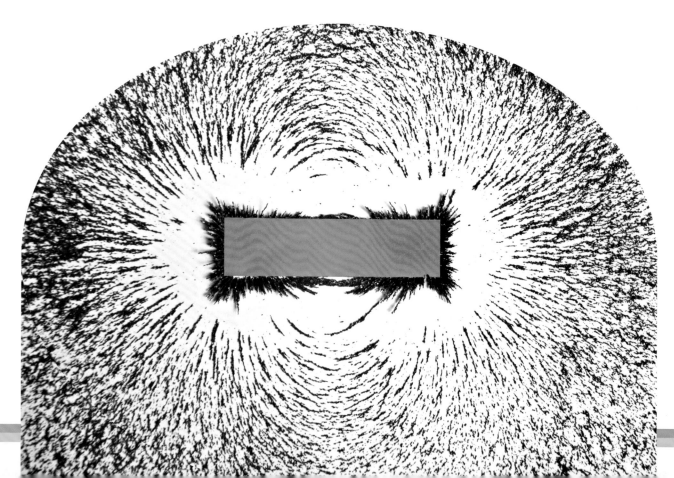

Finding magnetic fields

Scientists use machines called **magnetometers** to find magnetic fields and measure their strength. **Archaeologists** use magnetometers to find long-buried metal objects. **Astronomers** use them to find magnetic fields in space.

A bomb-disposal expert searches for **landmines** using a magnetometer. It can detect the magnetic field around any metal mines hidden underground.

Place a bar magnet on a sheet of paper or card. Drop paperclips near it. Move the magnet around. Watch the paperclips jump to the ends of the magnet. Some form chains between the two poles of the magnet.

The Earth is a magnet

The Earth has its own magnetic field. It is as if it has a huge bar magnet inside it. Like all magnets, it attracts magnetic materials, especially iron or steel.

A compass

A **compass** is a dial with a magnetic needle. The Earth's magnetic field pulls the needle, so that it always points from north to south. Sailors have used compasses for hundreds of years to help them find their way across the sea, where there are no **landmarks** to guide them.

Study a compass. You will see how it always points from north to south – unless you bring a magnet close to it. What happens then?

To find out where north is, move the compass until the marked point of the needle is pointing at the 'N'. Then the W, E and S will show where west, east and south are.

Ancient science

People made the first compasses around 1,000 years ago, from a kind of magnetic rock called **lodestone**. Sailors in Europe and in China discovered that if they let a piece of lodestone swing freely, it always ended up pointing north to south. It was a simple compass. Later, people learned to make compasses with iron needles.

This is a copy of a Chinese ship from the 1400s. It is like a ship from the fleet of a famous admiral called Zheng-He. He sailed from China to Africa, India and Arabia, and was one of the first sailors to use a compass to find the way.

Make a compass

You will need:

A sewing needle around 2 cm long, a small bar magnet, a small piece of flat **polystyrene** cut from the base of a cup, sticky tape, a saucer and some water.

You can make a simple compass using an ordinary sewing needle.
The needle is made of steel, which is a magnetic material.
You'll need to know which direction is north before you start.

First, magnetise the needle.
Use a bar magnet. Stroke the needle with one end of your magnet at least 25 times. Always use the same end of the magnet. Always stroke it in the same direction.

Tape the needle to the polystyrene.

1

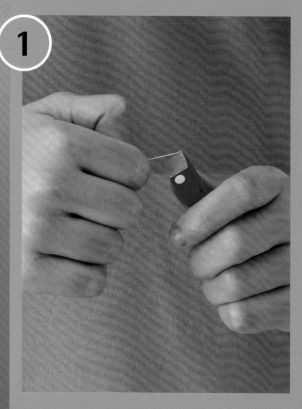

2

18

Fill a saucer with water. Gently, place the polystyrene and needle on the water. Leave it for a little while. What happens?

3

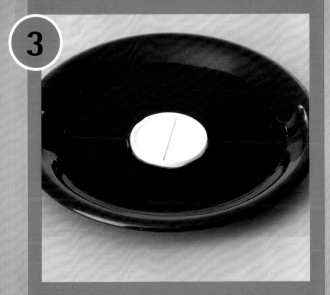

If you have made your needle into a strong enough magnet, the Earth's magnetic field will always make it point from north to south. Your needle is acting as a compass. You can check its accuracy by looking at a real compass.

Try moving the polystyrene, so that the needle no longer points north to south. Let it go, and watch how it will always go back to pointing north to south. This is because the Earth's magnetic force is acting on it, just as it acts on the needle of a normal compass.

4

What happens?

Try placing a bar magnet near your compass needle and watch what happens. What happens when you take the magnet away?

Electromagnets

It is possible to make magnets that we can turn on and off. We can do this using electricity.

How it is made

Around 200 years ago, a Danish scientist called Hans Oersted noticed that a wire carrying an electric current made a compass needle move. The wire worked as a magnet. Later, scientists found that the magnet is stronger if wire is coiled around a piece of iron. The more coils there are, the stronger the magnet is. This kind of magnet is called an **electromagnet**.

This picture shows Hans Oersted (left) and other scientists, experimenting with electricity and magnetism.

Using electromagnets

An ordinary magnet is called a **permanent magnet**. It works all the time. An electromagnet only works when an electric current is running through it. Electromagnets can be used to lift scrap metal, and drop it in the right place, when the power is switched off. Electromagnets are also used in some scientific equipment, such as **MRI** (Magnetic Resonance Imaging) scanners in hospitals. These can show what is happening inside a human body.

An electromagnet being used to lift and move scrap metal. As soon as the electric current is turned off, the metal falls away from the magnet.

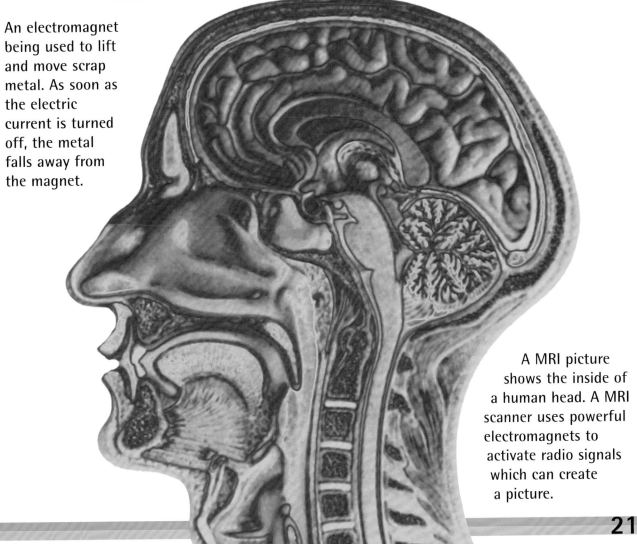

A MRI picture shows the inside of a human head. A MRI scanner uses powerful electromagnets to activate radio signals which can create a picture.

Make an electromagnet

It is possible to make a small electromagnet yourself, and see how magnetism can be turned on and off. In this experiment, we suggest you use a screwdriver, but a large nail will do as well.

You will need:

A long piece of thin, insulated wire; a small screwdriver with a non-magnetic tip and a metal shaft; a battery (6 volts or 4.5); a roll of **insulating tape**; a sharp blade (and an adult to use this); paperclips.

Tape one end of the wire to the handle of the screwdriver, with a little of the wire on the handle side hanging free.

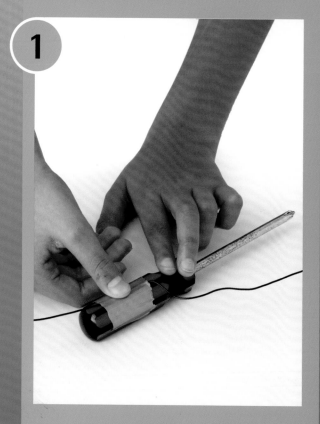

Wind the wire around the screwdriver, and, when you have finished winding, fasten the wire in place with the insulating tape. Make sure there is some wire left free at this end, too.

Scrape the insulation off the ends of the wire. Ask an adult to help with this, as you will need a sharp blade. Attach these ends of the wire to the battery, using the tape.

Move the screwdriver towards the paperclips and see what happens. Then remove the wire from the battery and see what happens.

3

4

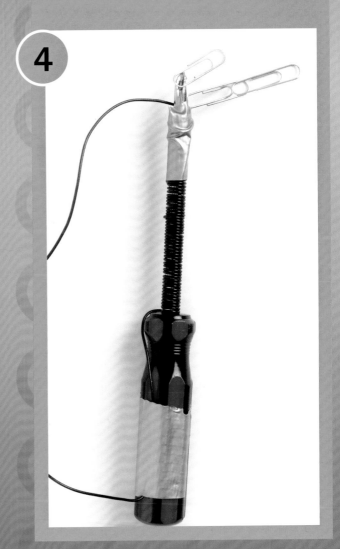

Now try this

Can you think of a way to make a switch, so you can turn your magnet on and off?

Electric motors

Electromagnets are used in electric motors. These are used to power many machines, both inside our homes and outside them.

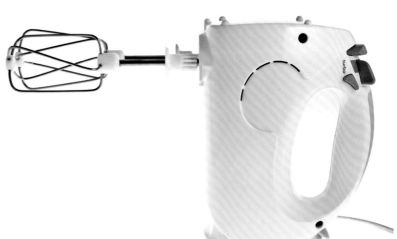

How it works

In an electric motor, an electromagnet, called an **armature**, sits between the two permanent magnets. The armature is made so that it can spin. When the power is on, the two permanent magnets and the armature all exert magnetic forces. The push and pull of these forces make the armature spin very fast. This makes the motor work.

Electric whisks (above) and food processors (below) contain simple electric motors that make the blades spin around.

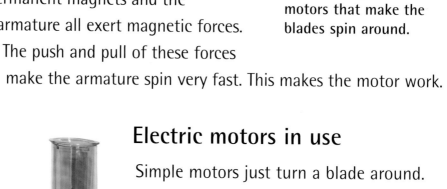

Electric motors in use

Simple motors just turn a blade around. This is how electric fans work, as well as mixers, coffee-grinders, washing machines and lawn-mowers. In an electric drill, the motor turns the drill bit. Powerful electric motors can make vehicles move, including electric cars and trains.

Electric trains get the electricity they need for their motors from cables above the ground, or from a rail on the ground. Some can travel at over 250 km an hour.

An electric car uses a powerful battery to store the electricity it needs to run its motor.

Maglev trains

Some modern trains, called **maglev trains**, work using the power of magnets to attract and repel. They use electromagnets, which can be turned on when the train is running, and off to make the train stop.

How they work

A maglev train runs using powerful magnets in the track, which is called a **guideway**. These are for **'levitation'** (lifting). The magnets exert a force that repels another set of magnets under the train. They make the train hover above the guideway. Many maglev trains also have another set of magnets that pull them along the guideway. Others use jet engines instead.

A record-breaking Japanese maglev train, which travels at high speed – almost silently.

Floating along

A maglev train's wheels are only used when it slows down and stops. While it is on the move, it floats. This makes the ride very smooth. Maglev trains are often used in airports to carry passengers for short distances. But they are also used over long-distances. In Japan, test runs of maglev trains have reached speeds of nearly 600 km an hour.

Passengers at some airports travel between terminals on maglev trains that run every few minutes. This train is at Munich airport.

Experiment with two bar magnets on a shiny surface. Can you get one magnet to move without them touching each other?

Making electricity

Hans Oersted found out that we can use electricity to make a magnet. This works the other way around, too. It is possible to make electricity using magnets. This is how electricity is **generated** in **power stations**.

How it works

In the 1820s, two scientists, Michael Faraday, in Britain, and Joseph Henry, in the USA, both discovered the same thing. They found that spinning a magnet inside a wire makes electricity flow through the wire. Power stations do this on a large scale. The magnets in power stations are made to spin using wheels called **turbines**.

Steam is often used to turn the turbines in a power station. Here, we can see it rising high into the air after it has been used.

Spinning the turbines

Many power stations burn coal, oil or gas to make steam, and this turns the turbines. Heat from **nuclear energy** can also be used to make steam. All these methods create pollution. But some power stations use moving water to turn turbines. Others use giant wind turbines. Wind and water can be used to generate electricity without creating pollution.

The wind makes the blades of these turbines spin. This works a generator, to create electricity.

There are turbines inside this dam. As water pours over them, they spin and generate electricity.

Glossary

archaeologist Someone who studies the remains of people and objects from distant times.

armature An electromagnet that is part of an electric motor.

astronomer A scientist who studies the stars, planets and space.

cobalt A silvery, magnetic metal.

compass A dial with a magnetic needle that always points north/south.

domain The tiny parts of a magnet.

electromagnet A magnet made by coiling wire around a metal rod and running an electric current through the wire.

electronic equipment Gadgets or machines that use the same kind of system as a computer.

force A push or a pull. The force of a magnet is called magnetism.

generate To make. We say that electricity is generated in a power station.

guideway The pathway a maglev train runs on.

insulating tape Sticky tape that does not allow electricity to pass through it.

iron filings Tiny pieces of iron.

landmark Something we recognise, such as a building, that helps us know where we are.

landmine An explosive device hidden underground that explodes when stepped on or driven over.

levitation Lifting. Magnetic levitation makes the maglev trains hover above the track.

lines of force Invisible lines in a magnetic field that spread out from a magnet's north to the south poles.

lodestone A kind of rock containing magnetised material.

maglev A kind of train that runs using the power of magnets to keep it above the ground.

magnetic field The area around a magnet where its force can be felt.

magnetic material Any material that a magnet can attract.

magnetise Make a material into something that has magnetic force.

magnetometer A scientific instrument that measures magnetic forces.

MRI (Magnetic Resonance Imaging) an instrument used in hospitals that uses magnets to activate radio signals. These can make a picture of what is happening inside a body.

nickel A silvery magnetic metal.

nuclear energy Powerful energy released by changes in atoms, which are the tiny particles from which all materials are made.

permanent magnet A magnet that keeps its magnetism all the time.

pole One or other end of a magnet.

polystyrene A kind of light plastic.

power station A building that contains the machinery for making electricity.

repel Drive or push away.

steam Water in the form of a vapour or gas.

steel Iron mixed with carbon.

turbine A wheel that turns the machinery used to make electricity.

Some answers

page 7: The magnet will work through paper. It will probably work through card, too, but this depends on how strong the magnet is, and how thick the card is.

Page 11: Even though they are not straight pieces of metal, horseshoe magnets each have a north pole (at the end of one 'arm') and one south pole (at the end of the other). If you hold the magnets so that the north and south poles are opposite each other, you will feel the force of the magnet trying to attract them together. But you hold them so that the two north poles and two south poles are opposite each other, you will feel the magnets trying to repel each other.

Page 13: The distance you can move the magnet from the paperclip without the paperclip falling back to the bottom of the jar depends on the strength of the magnet.

Page 15: If the paperclips are made of magnetic material, they will cluster around the ends of the magnet. They may form chains, looping between the ends of the magnet – in the same way that the iron filings in the picture on page 14 formed loops between the poles of the magnet. This illustrates the lines of force around a magnet.

Page 16: If you bring a magnet close to a compass needle, the needle will move away from the north and towards the magnet. This is because the magnet is nearby and exerts a stronger magnetic force than the Earth.

Page 19: As with a proper compass, a magnet will affect the way the needle points on your home-made compass. The south pole of your compass needle will be drawn to the north pole of the bar magnet. When you take the magnet away, the needle will return to pointing to the north.

Page 27: When you bring one magnet towards another, the opposite poles are attracted to each other and the free one will be drawn towards the magnet you are holding. If you place two like poles opposite each other, you will see the free magnet slide away for a short distance, and then swing around.

Index

Further information

www.bbc.co.uk/schools/ks2bitesize/science/
revision_bites/magnets_springs.shtml
Basic facts about magnets at KS2.

http://van.physics.uiuc.edu/qa/listing.php?
id=12497
More basic facts about magnets.

www.newi.ac.uk/buckleyc/magnet.htm
More complicated background information about
magnets and their history.

http://science.howstuffworks.com/magnet.htm
How magnets work.

http://www.edfenergy.com/about-us/energy-
generation/story-power-generation.shtml
About generating electricity.

http://education.jlab.org/qa/electromagnet.html
More about making an electromagnet.

http://resources.schoolscience.co.uk/CDA/14-
16/physics/copch3pg1.html
How an electric motor works.

http://science.howstuffworks.com/
maglev-train.htm
How a maglev train works.

Note to parents and teachers: Every effort has been made by
the Publishers to ensure that these websites are suitable for
children, that they are of the highest educational value, and
that they contain no inappropriate or offensive material.
However, because of the nature of the Internet, it is impossible
to guarantee that the contents of these sites will not be
altered. We strongly advise that Internet access is supervised
by a responsible adult.